Getting Back Together

The Secret to Seduce and Make Your Ex to Fall in Love With You Again

Deanna M. Roberts

Copyright

ISBN: 978-1-304-99451-6

Terms of Use

This book is intended solely for dispensing of information of an educational value for the purpose of helping those who read it to restore a failed personal relationship. Application of the information within is recommended in line with a rational and responsible approach to your individual circumstance. Readers are cautioned to reply on their own judgment about their individual circumstances to act accordingly.

This book is not intended for use as a source of legal, psychological or counselling advice. All readers are advised to seek services of competent professionals in legal, business, accounting, and finance field.

If you use the information within to assist with repairing your damaged relationship, the author and publisher assume no responsibility for the results of your actions.

Contents

1. Introduction

All good things must end and that includes relationships. There are numerous reasons why a relationship ends and all of them are hurtful. When a relationship has ended, and when the hurt fades, sometimes you realize that you want that person back. Just because your relationship ended does not mean that you cannot win your ex back.

There are second chances and when you do it right, you can win your ex back and rebuild your relationship, making it stronger and better than ever. A second relationship with someone is another chance to get it right, and this time, you have the advantage of already knowing where it went wrong the first time so you can take the appropriate steps to get it right the second time around. Mistakes are only failures if you fail to learn from them.

Every mistake from your prior relationship is an opportunity to change and to grow. By doing so, you can avoid making the same mistakes over and over again. First of all, if you are reading this book with the mindset that you had no part to play in why your relationship failed, this book will not be able to help you. It takes two to make a relationship work and it takes two to heal it.

If you have the attitude that it was all the other person's fault and that you do not need to change, this is not the book for you. This book is about embracing your mistakes and turning them into another opportunity. This is about correcting the wrongs and building a solid relationship based on two people who want to be together and are willing to give and take as needed.

There are three ways that a relationship ends; they end it, you end it, or it is a mutual decision. No matter who ended it, it is possible for you to win back your ex. By examining your relationship, yourself, and your ex, you can win them back.

2. Why Did It End?

It does not matter if you ended things, if they ended things, or if you came to a mutual agreement to end the relationship; you need to know why it ended. Unless you can pinpoint why the relationship ended, you will not be able to take the necessary steps needed to fix things. You cannot win your ex back unless you can offer a better relationship than the first time around.

Lots of advice columns and blogs suggest that the way to get your ex back is by working on your appearance. They suggest that you change your wardrobe, lose weight, and focus on your own appearance.

There is merit in some of that, but only because when you feel good about how you look and feel, your self-esteem is boosted and so is your confidence. Your looks did not end the relationship and if so, do you really want them back if the relationship is based solely on how you look?

This book is not focused on fluff. Any suggestions made about appearance are given to help you feel better about yourself, not as a way to fix a relationship. No healthy relationship is based on looks. If you feel that physical appearance played a major role in why your relationship ended, you need to dig deeper.

Why did it end? What role did each of you play in the ending of the relationship? Not all relationships ended on a bad note because of something like infidelity. Sometimes, it is just a combination of many smaller things.

When you analyze your relationship to determine why it ended, it means you have to ask yourself some tough questions. You cannot only focus on what the other person did, you also have to examine your total relationship, including your own actions and reactions.

What are some of the reasons that relationship ended? Think back to your relationship and your arguments and discussions. What frustrated you the most about the other person? What about you frustrated them the most? All relationships have to be balanced and when that balance is tipped too far one way or another, it will fail.

Not Enough Value Placed on the Relationship

One reason that relationships fail is because someone did not value the other person. When you take someone for granted, it hurts. Indifference will destroy a relationship faster than anger. If you treated your partner with indifference, they will only suffer through that for so long.

How much did you value your relationship? Did you realize how much they meant to you after they were gone? Chances are, you did. If you value them now, why did you not value them before?

Relationships take work; anything that you value takes work. If you do not work for your relationship, it shows that you did not value it.

It Became Boring

No one loves boring. Even long-term relationships should be fresh feeling and exciting. When you fall into a rut that you do not try to break out of, your partner will look for that fresh, fun feeling elsewhere.

What attracted you to them originally? How did that spark of attraction feel? If you do not try to recapture that feeling throughout your relationship, it will become boring.

Insecurity

Everyone has insecurities but when you let your insecurities manifest as neediness and clingy behavior, it will drive your partner away. No one wants to have somebody clinging to him or her, acting like a shadow, or tracking his or her every move.

To you, you are trying to show them that you care but to them, you are keeping tabs on them and it translates to a lack of trust on your part. We all want to be valued but you cannot demand it from them or it comes through as being needy and clingy. Neither have any place in a healthy relationship.

Jealousy is another way in which your insecurity can manifest. If you are suspicious of their every action, why would they stay? You need to trust them just as they need to trust you. If you cannot trust someone, then you should not be in a relationship with them. Jealousy is something that needs to be overcome in favor of healthier emotions.

Drifting Apart

Have you ever tried to be friendly with someone who just did not like you? If you are so fiercely independent that you come off as distant and uninterested, they will stop trying. If you let your ego rule your actions and emotions, you will find that you drift apart because you will be putting up so many walls up to keep others out that they cannot connect with you. Your partner needs to connect with you, and when you do not let them, it will cause the relationship to dissolve.

Being Too Critical and Nagging

If what you have to say is not constructive criticism, you should stay silent. Being too critical, often just to argue, is a major relationship mistake. No one wants to be nagged and judged. Breakdown in communications is another major cause of relationships ending. Learn how to communicate better to overcome this.

Once you begin to realize why the relationship ended, you can begin to formulate a plan to get them back. This requires a lot of work on your end because you have to genuinely want to improve yourself to correct the mistakes that you made in the relationship. Without change, there can be no healing and no success.

3. Do You Really Want Back Together?

This is the big question. Do you really want back together or do you just think you do? When a breakup is fresh, it is easy to feel like you must have them back but then on the second try, the same problems come up. Some relationships are just not healthy so you need to determine if you really want to go back to them.

If you are still angry or hurt, you need to be able to let that go. If you try to get back together but you want to hold their mistakes over their head constantly, that is not going to work. That is counterproductive. If you think that you can move on from the bad times to start over, then trying again is a good idea. Only you know how badly you were hurt and if you can move past it or not.

A second chance means that you need to forgive. Forgiveness is not always easy when you have been hurt but if you really want back together, you must forgive them for what they have done. That does not mean that you have to tolerate them doing it again!

If you are willing to take them back knowing you will get hurt again, you do not belong back together. This book is about promoting ways to get your ex back for a healthy relationship.

Everyone has value and if you are not being treated right, get out of the relationship. Do not be a doormat for someone who does not appreciate you. Your well-being is more important than your relationship.

If you want them back because you feel that you cannot find anyone else, and are willing to let them treat you poorly, getting back together is not recommended. Relationships should not be a power play, it should be an even flow of power.

If that is what you want, then you should get back together because it means you can set your ego aside while not sacrificing your own identity. You also have to be able to forgive yourself for your part in the breakup.

If you constantly berate yourself for any hurt you caused them, it will work against you. People make mistakes, but as long as you are willing to work on yourself, to correct your mistakes, then you should be able to forgive yourself and move forward with winning your ex back.

Are you willing to change? If you are willing to give them a chance to change and learn from their mistakes, are you willing to do the same? You cannot expect them to do all of the work. You have to really want to improve so that you can help heal the relationship. If you make the same mistakes, your relationship will have the same result as before; it will end. Your willingness to change is a big factor in if you want to get back together.

You need to take into account what your role in the relationship was and what their role was. One thing to consider is that you miss the relationship more than you miss your ex. If that is the case, then you confusing being lonely, or missing the comfort of being in a relationship, with love.

If you want to get your ex back just to end the pain of being alone, then you should not get back together. If you want your ex back because you cannot imagine your life without them, moving forward with getting them back is a good idea. Keep in mind that this only works if you both want this to work, which means moving forward from your past.

If things ended on such a bad note that there is no civility between the two of you, getting back together is a tall order. If your relationship has more bad memories than pleasant ones, do you really want to venture into that territory again?

The best relationships to reconcile with are the ones that started off good and then fell apart. When you have a good basis to start from, it is easier to find common ground with your ex, based on the good times. If your relationship was in constant turmoil from day one, it will be harder to find a good, solid basis to get your ex back. Only you know in your heart if you truly want your ex back and if the answer is yes, keep reading.

4. Desperation is a Turn Off

When you are trying to seduce your ex to win them back, the worst thing you can do is appear needy and desperate. No matter how much you were in the wrong, begging them to come back to you is not the way to go. The more desperate you act, the harder you will make it to seduce your ex.

Remember, the key is to make them fall in love with you all over again, to build a better relationship. Begging and pleading and acting desperate is the ultimate turn off.

For example, you want them back badly. That desperation turns into borderline obsession. You find yourself calling, texting, emailing, or even trying to see them constantly. There is nothing positive or seductive about desperation. Throwing yourself upon their mercy to take you back is a cliché; it only works in the movies. Histrionics and begging is not only not dignified but it is also not very seductive.

You want to seduce your ex, to show them that you are the one for them and that you can fix the relationship, making it better than ever. You do not want to turn into a pest, begging for another chance.

When you want someone badly, and you are trying to atone for mistakes, you know you have an uphill battle. However, it is a battle that can be won!

When you are needy, it forces the other person to focus only on that. You want them to focus on your positives, not your negatives.

Desperation pushes them away and what you want is to pull them in. You want to show them why getting back together with you is a good thing. You want them to realize that you are the one. If you are needy and desperate now, that is a sign that you will be that way during the entire relationship. When you act desperately, you are shooting yourself in the foot and sabotaging your chances of getting back together.

A lot of the time, you are needy because you feel a sense of urgency about getting back together. You want to get back together with them before they find someone else. Guess what? It does not matter! Let them date around and you know why? Because it gives you time to shine! Stop being in a rush to get them back; it is good to let a little bit of time go by before getting back together. In fact, it is recommended.

That might seem like it is going against the grain of the topic of the book. If you want to seduce your ex, why would you want them to date other people? You want them to date others because, they are hurt over the end of the relationship too and this allows them to get past that. In the prior chapter, the topic of forgiveness was brought up. You need to be able to forgive them for their actions to be a couple again.

That goes both ways. To see you in a positive light and to want to be together with you again, they need to be able to forgive you. If you rush right back into a relationship, they will not have had time to go through the necessary emotional steps to get over grief or anger and it will work against you. You need to have a period of no contact, where you each go about your lives. However, during this stage, you are actually continually working toward getting your ex back.

Letting them date other people without throwing jealous fits is necessary. Not only does it show that you are mature enough to see them move on, but it also allows them to work through their own feelings. You want them to have the time to do this. If that means they date around a little bit, fine. All the better because when you make your move, you will be back, better than ever before, ready to show them why they want and need to come back to you.

This means you do not blame them for the breakup, you do not constantly ask them to get back together with you, you do not pester them with apologies, you do not contact them daily, and you give them space.

When you can pull your focus back from getting back together with your ex, it will work out much better for you in the long run. Your life should not center around them when you were together so it should not center around them when you are trying to get back together either.

Your goal is to work on being the type of person who they enjoy talking to, and enjoy being around. You do not need to shove memories of all of the good times you had down their throats because you are going to do something better, you are going to give them time and space and then you are going to re-enter their lives and give them whole new memories.

You are not going to just pick up where you had left off, you are going to be a whole new you, one who will be irresistible to them. Seduce, not beg.

5. Things to Avoid

Before going into how to seduce your ex, you need to know what not to do. These are the behaviors that will make it impossible for you to seduce him or her to win him or her back.

This chapter is dedicated to the common mistakes people make when trying to seduce their ex. To win them back, you have to show them why they want to be with you, not remind them of why they broke up with you in the first place! These are the things you need to avoid doing to win your ex back.

Acting Like a Victim

Do not act like a victim by pointing out all the things that they did to you during the relationship. The relationship ended because of actions on both of your parts, so leave the victim routine at home. If you try to manufacture reasons for them to be sympathetic toward you, it will not work. Stop throwing yourself a pity party and they'll want to spend more time with you but when you willingly put yourself into a victim mentality, it will work against you.

If you try to act pitiful, to get them to feel sorry for you, it will backfire. People do not want to enter into a relationship with someone who is acting like a victim. There is a big difference between creating an air of mystery about yourself and trying to win them back with sympathy. By trying to make them feel sorry for you, you will not be doing yourself any favors and it will backfire on you.

Actions Speak Louder Than Words

Naturally, there were problems that caused your relationship to end the first time around. To win your ex back, you need to change so that you can be a better relationship partner. One of the biggest mistakes people make is that they keep talking about how much they have changed but they do not show it.

Let your actions speak louder than words; show them the new you. Show them how far you have come in the way of improving. They will see the changes and be willing to take a risk to get back together. If you do nothing but talk about your changes, it will sound like a lot of hot air and empty promises.

You need to prove that you are better, not tell them. Only through your actions can you convince them that you are the partner they want and you will win them back.

Drop the Mind Games

This should go without saying, but still, some people try to manipulate their ex by playing mind games. If you are not 100% sure you and your ex belong together, do not try to get back together with them.

This book is only for the people who are serious about getting back together with their ex for a long-term relationship. If you are not sure, then do not try. Mind games have no place in a relationship, especially not a second chance relationship.

Always Be Honest

Honesty is always the best policy, especially when you are trying to get your ex back. During the process of getting your ex back, at some point, your past relationship and your feelings will need to be discussed. A small lie told in the early stages of getting back together will destroy your relationship later.

You need to be honest at all times and if you find that you need to say something that could possibly be hurtful, find a way to say them without being emotional, without placing blame, and without lying. Lying is a sign that you cannot be trusted. You want them to be honest with you, so you must always be honest with them.

Do Not Be Pushy

Seducing your ex to win them back is a long process. It cannot be rushed unless you want to risk having this fail. Winning your ex back is a delicate process, one with many steps, and it takes time. They need time to process what is going on and you each need time to grow, plus time to begin to heal, and then finally, it takes time to rebuild your relationship. If you try to push them to commit earlier than they are ready to, it will backfire.

You cannot be pushy and you cannot demand that they make a decision one way or another too quickly. You do not want to force them into dating you again, you want them to want to be with you and that is why you slowly seduce them into being with you again. Take it slow, let them take their time to decide, and you will get them back.

Do Not Be Flirty Too Soon

Naturally, you want to be flirty to win them back but not during the opening stages. Go for friendly, not flirty, because you want to build up to being flirty later on. You have to be patient to get them back. Wait until you are spending more time together and that the dynamic between the two of you is good again before you begin being flirty.

Do Not Involve Family and Friends

This is not a sports match; you are going to win them back on your own merits, not by trying to influence their decision through family and friends. For example, if they are not responding to your initial attempts at reaching out, do not go to their friends and family to pass on messages for you. You will get them back on your own, so that means that you leave your mutual friends and their friends and their family out of it.

Watch What You Say

Whatever you say to others will always have a way of getting back to whomever you are talking about. If you are badmouthing your ex, even to your own friends, it will eventually get back to them.

Plus, when you do get them back and your friends give them the cold shoulder because of all the negative things you said about them, it will be uncomfortable for them and they could end up ending any budding second relationship with you over it.

Always speak kindly of them, never criticize or judge. This is especially hard if they are dating someone else. Do not speak ill of whomever they are dating. It will get back to your ex that you are saying unpleasant things about who they are dating. Is that the image you want to project? No, so always be mindful of what you say about them and keep it possible.

Dating is Good But Not Their Friends

Part of getting on with our life is that you should date others, just casual dating for fun but do not date their friends! That will kill any chance you have of getting them back! When you do this, it comes off as being spiteful.

6. Road to Recovery

The road to relationship recovery is where you begin to make the first steps toward getting your ex back. This often includes you needing to take a long, hard look at what your faults are so you can fix them. This is the time for you to focus on you, and not on them. You cannot seduce them if you are still making all the same mistakes and this is your chance to correct them.

The road to recovery is you taking care of you and your needs so that you can be a better partner. All too often, the focus toward getting your ex back is so consuming that it takes over your life. When you let it take over your life, everyone knows about it and everyone sees it, including your ex.

They will not get back together with you if you are obsessing over them, because that just puts the relationship on rocky ground to begin with. No, you need to start taking steps to work on yourself first.

First of all, get rid of your resentments toward them. Even if they hurt you, if you want to get back together, you have to let that go. Letting it go means that you stop dwelling on all of the negatives, the bad parts, and the hurt. It means that you do not complain to your family and friends about the breakup, or about your ex. Bitterness is no way to begin recovering.

In fact, the less you say to anyone about the breakup or about your ex, the better your chances will be of getting your ex back. Take the high road and say nothing negative, derogatory, or vengeful. This earns you brownie points right away.

How easy do you think it will be to get back to your ex if you are writing negative things about them on your social media sites or when you talk to others?

Be mindful of what you say about the breakup and about your ex. Say nothing that you would not want to say directly to your ex. That way, your words will not be able to come back and haunt you later on, when you are trying to get back together with your ex. Harboring and feeding negative emotions will not help you recover, and it will only harm your ability to get your ex back.

Another tendency is to sit at home and feel sorry for yourself. Isolating yourself is not healthy. Your ex will not take you back if you become a hermit, hiding in the shadows of your house or apartment. You need to show them that you are someone worth being with and that your life is worth sharing with them and so you need to have a life post-breakup.

Stop whining about the break up and how much you miss them or want them back. Your family and friends are very much aware that you broke up; you do not need to go over and over it again and again like a broken record. Everyone knows you are upset and you have a right to be but that does not mean you are allowed to endlessly complain about it.

Instead of complaining about it, do something about it! So, leave the pity party and the whining for others, you get one or two days to feel sorry for yourself and no more. After that, you stop complaining, you stop crying, and you start getting on with things in your life.

You can only mourn your lost relationship for a little bit, just a day or two and then you have to pull yourself up and get yourself on the road to relationship recovery. What part did you play in the break up?

Were you jealous and clingy because you have low self-esteem? Did you cheat? Did you act too distant or just take them for granted? Whatever role you played, you now have a chance to fix.

This is your period of transformation to the new you. During this time, you do not contact your ex; the next chapter will go into that in more detail but it bears mentioning them. You and your ex should not have contact if you can help it, no matter how badly you want to. This period of time is necessary for you to redefine yourself into a better partner.

Turn your break up into a positive by improving yourself. Everyone has room for improvement; look at your break up as a blessing in disguise because now you know what you need to work on. If you do not go into this phase with an open mind and a heart willing to change, you will not be able to win your ex back. You have to understand that you need to fix your flaws to seduce your ex.

Self-improvement is a positive thing. Do it not only to get your ex back but also to make yourself happier. You will find that the changes you make will not only help you get your ex back but it will also help all of your relationships, such as with family, friends, and at work.

You are working not only to get your ex back but also to make your life easier by being a better person. You are reinventing yourself from this point forward because the point is to seduce your ex based on how you are now, the new you.

Take your negative traits, the ones that contributed to the end of the relationship and begin working to eliminate them. If you had a habit of never letting them speak, learn to use restraint and let others finish what they are saying.

Here is an exercise that will show you exactly how your past behaviors were damaging to the relationship. Give a friend a list of all of the things that you think you did to help end the relationship and have them do those things to you.

For example, if you nagged them, have your friend nag you. If you were distant or did not value your relationship, have your friend turn a cold shoulder to you or take your for granted. When the tables are turned on you, it is easy to understand that you have undesirable traits that need to be addressed. Start working on them!

Self-esteem and self-confidence are two of the hardest to overcome. The best way to boost your self-esteem is by loving yourself. If you are deeply unhappy with how you look, freshen your wardrobe, try a new hairstyle, or just take up some exercise.

Taking care of yourself and your health feels good. It is for you, not them. Take this time to pamper yourself, do the things you like, and make sure that you go out and have fun.

7. Give Them Space

You want them back and your first instinct will be to tell them that. Resist! You need to institute a no contact policy for at least three to four weeks. If they contact you, naturally, you want to talk to them and that is okay. If they contact you, do not gush about missing them or begging to go back together, just play it cool. Ask how they have been and make small talk.

Patience, remember! If they contact you first, it makes things so much easier and often, during this no contact period, they just might.

When you give them space, it gives you both time to digest the break up. It allows for the bad feelings to even out, and for anger to ebb away. They hurt you, you hurt them, and no relationship can ever be re-kindled when there are still embers of anger and resentment burning. You need to give them space to let go of their negative emotions.

Giving them space also prevents you from blowing your chances of seducing them back into your life by being needy. It cannot be stressed enough that being needy is never a good thing and when you want to get your ex back, it can be a huge problem.

To you, they are your other half and you are trying to convince them to come back, but to them, you are clinging and they do not want to go down that dark road of neediness and jealousy again. This period of no contact is for their benefit and for yours.

Another reason to give them space is because they will begin to miss you. If you keep contacting them, they will not have any time to really miss you but if you cut all contact, they will find that their mind keeps wandering back to you and the relationship.

Perhaps they expected you to cry and take it badly or that you might beg them to come back. When you do none of these things, they begin to think that they underestimated you and that perhaps they should not have even broke up with you.

We value things much more after they are gone from our lives. Taking yourself out of their life gives them time to dwell on the break up and the relationship and they will begin to realize that they valued it and miss it.

Seduction is partially a power play, and by giving them time, you are actually putting the power into your own hands.

Getting through this period of no contact is sometimes hard. This is where many people end up failing because they let a week go by and they feel that one week is enough. It is not. If you want to keep the balance of power shifted in your favor, you have to go a minimum of three weeks without initiating contact with them. So, how can you go about that?

You must understand that your relationship with them is over. It has ended. You are not trying to salvage that same relationship; it is gone so stop thinking as if it is not over. You want to seduce them and start a new relationship. Let go of that dead relationship.

Until you admit to yourself that it is over, you will not be able to succeed. If you cannot let go of the relationship, you will always be pulled back into your past and that means that you are not future focused. You need to focus on your future, on getting your ex back and forging a new relationship.

Now, it is time to start being single. This will help you get your ex out of your mind and out of your life for the time being. Do not worry, this is not permanent, just for the no contact period but these are steps that will help you get through this time without breaking down and calling or texting them.

Pull out your cell phone and write down their number, his address, etc. Whatever ways you have of contacting your ex, write it all down on a piece of paper and then put it in an envelope and seal it. Label the envelope with their name and then put it somewhere where you will not forget about it but where it is not where you can see it daily.

Now, delete them from your phone and email. Delete them as a phone contact and from your email address book. You will not be able to give into the urge to pull out your phone and contact them. You can keep them on social media, but only if you can restrain yourself from checking their pages. If you cannot stop yourself from checking their pages, you need to unfriend them or unfollow them to keep you from constantly checking their page.

If you have pictures of the two of you up, take them down. If you have things that remind you of them, such as gifts that came from them and you associate with them, put them all in a box. You are getting rid of all of the things that will make you melancholy. Just store the box in storage, in your attic, your garage, or in the back of a closet but do not look into it. If you cannot resist opening the box, give it to a family member to hold onto.

The above steps will help you greatly when it comes to getting through the next three to four weeks of no contact.

8. Focus on You

As much as you want your ex back, you need to spend some time focusing on you. What do you think your ex will value more, you falling over yourself trying to please them or you going on with your life, holding yourself together and acting like an adult?

When you focus on you, you are playing hard to get, which means that you value yourself above all else. When you carry on about getting them back or about the ended relationship, it is not mature behavior.

Relationships are mature things, if you act immaturely after the breakup, it reflects badly on you. If you act as if you are hurt but going on with things, accepting the break up and moving forward, it shows maturity.

Maturity is a must for any relationship. You want to seduce your ex and win them back by showing them how you have grown as person and that the things you did not offer in the relationship before, you are ready to offer now. You will be showing that you have value.

Playing hard to get means you value yourself. It also makes your ex value you more. They might have expected you to pull some sort of hysterical antics about getting back together and when you do not do it, they will be pleasantly surprised. This is always a way to test the waters to see if they are interested in getting back together. The only way to win your ex back is through gentle seduction, not an all-out assault.

You must seduce them into seeing your value as a partner. Flinging yourself at them, the all-out assault tactic, is not a good ploy. They will just shake off your efforts and be glad that they are done with you. Show them what they are missing and they will start to miss what the two of you had together. That is why, right after the breakup, you need to focus only on yourself.

Take care to not fall into the cycle of depression. You cannot seduce your ex back into your life if you are sitting on the couch, crying and eating ice cream. You need to be vivacious and full of life, you have to highlight all of your positives while working extra hard to get rid of your negative traits.

This is the fake it and make it tactic for overcoming the grief stage of the relationship. You might not be happy inside but the happier you act, even if pretending, the happier you will actually end up being. Yes, by faking happiness, it actually helps you overcome depression to be happy.

Instead of isolating yourself in your house, go out and have fun with your friends. Go out and be seen. Chances are that you could use some time out with your friends so start going out. Movies, dinners, or just random fun, the point is to get out of the house and start smiling.

Your smile is the sexiest thing about you. You want them to fall in love with your smile once again. Do not worry, even if they do not see you out and about, word will get back to them through friends and mutual friends.

This is where social media comes in handy, it will help them see that you are doing just fine. It was mentioned that you should keep them as social media friends, provided you can resist the temptation to contact them. Post pictures of you and your friends going out. Your positive posts will have a better effect on your ex than posting long, sad sob stories.

If you post negative things about them or your ended relationship, they will just unfriend you and that makes seducing them harder. Posting pictures of yourself going on with your life will get them to think that they miss the good times you had together. Once they start thinking of the good times you two shared, the wheel will be in motion for getting them back.

Very likely, you could use a self-esteem boost as well. Do something to pamper yourself. Get a manicure, a massage, a day at the spa, or a new haircut. Change your hairstyle or color for a whole new look. After all, a whole new you deserves a new look. Buy some new clothes, something colorful and bright, or a new pair of shoes, watch, or jewelry. The point is to spend your money on you and to feel good about it.

Speaking of feeling good, being healthy is a good way to help you feel great about yourself. Some books recommend losing weight so that you can show them what they are missing physically, but that is the wrong idea.

Is physical attraction important? Yes, but it does not make for a solid relationship. However, if you feel good about yourself, you will find that you are less needy, less jealous, and less controlling.

You do not want to win them back, only to start those damaging behaviors again, and those are all things that can be fixed by a self-esteem boost. They were with you before, so they were already physically attracted to you, so you do not have to worry about that, but you need to love your body and to feel good about yourself so you can be a better partner.

That is the only reason why you should start taking a few extra steps to boost your body image. Get your teeth whitened or swap out two or three fast food meals every week with something healthy. Get active. Exercise actually wards off depression, so if you are feeling depressed about the breakup, lace up your tennis shoes and take a walk.

When you exercise, your body releases endorphins, which help elevate your mood. Not only will exercise make you feel better about your body and make you healthier but it also makes you happier, something that we all need after a break up. You do not need to try a total body transformation, just enough exercise to help you lose a few extra pounds and to make yourself feel better.

Walking and hand weights at home will help you easily start to lose a few pounds and love yourself. Self-confidence is necessary because when you get back together, there is no room for error for the mistakes of the past such as clinging, neediness, and jealousy. Show them that you have grown for the better and be secure that they are with you and only with you because you know how valuable of a person and a partner that you really are.

9. Dating Others

If you are trying to seduce your ex, why would you date other people? The answer is simple; it actually helps making seducing your ex easier. When you date others, you are showing that you are not desperate to get them back, and playing hard to get is a plus because they will work harder at getting you back, which is just what you want. Dating others also shows that you are confident in yourself, that you are still fun, and that you are moving on.

Take care to not go on more than a couple dates with the same person because you do not want to give the impression that you are dating someone else exclusively.

Go on dates with people who you can relax and have fun with, nothing that is going to be long term or even short term. That is why it is important to date around, not simply date one or two people repeatedly. You do not want to lead anyone else on, which is not the point.

Do not worry, you know that you are not moving on but your ex does not know that. You have moved on, from the past relationship with your ex, but not from your ex themselves. This is all a plan to get them back, and to do so, you need to date other people. Not only will it take your mind off of things and improve your own self-confidence, but it also is fun.

Desperation is never good, and when your ex sees you dating others, it will go in your favor when you are back in contact with them. If you were not dating others, they might be hesitant or worried when you finally do make contact, that it will be to whine and cry or, worse, blame them for the breakup.

By seeing that you are out there, dating others, you are obviously not going to be an emotion wreck when you talk to them and that is a good thing! Navigating your way back into your ex's life is not possible if talking to you is like walking through an emotional mine field. If they have to carefully weigh and measure each and every word before they say it to avoid setting you off, they would rather just avoid you totally than deal with that type of emotional burden.

However, when you are out dating others and moving on, your ex sees this and the worry that talking to you again will set off all sorts of negative emotional outbursts on your part will not happen. When they know that talking to you will not be a negative experience, it makes that first contact easier. If they do not see you dating others, they will worry that contact with you will be nothing more than a re-hashing of the ended relationship.

If you have moved on, there is nothing to re-hash because it is over and you are acting like it is over. By dating others, you are facilitating how easily your first post breakup contact with your ex will be.

Dating others is also a confidence booster. When a relationship ends, it is easy to blame the other person, and to blame yourself. It is common to feel that you are not loveable, not likeable, or not a good person. Getting back out there and casually dating others is a great way to get your self-esteem back. Go out, be flirty, and have fun.

It feels good to be wanted so go out, flirt, and go on dates with the people you meet. Casual dating boosts your self-esteem and because it is just one date, neither you nor the other person has any expectations that it will be anything more than a casual, fun night out on the town. Dating helps ease the pain and low self-esteem that comes after a breakup.

So, how do you start dating again? Go out with friends and just start talking to other single people around. Get phone numbers, then call back, and arrange for a date. You can meet a lot of people just by being out in public and having fun. Do not be afraid to go up and say hello to people. Being friendly is a great opener for a date.

Try online dating; there are numerous free online dating websites. Create a profile and list yourself as looking for casual dates and you will only be matched with other people who are looking for dates but no commitment. This is the best way because you both know from first contact that this is just a casual date, and that nothing that will turn serious.

It gets you out of the house, back into the dating world and it will help you get over the sting of the breakup. Your ex will see that you are moving on and it will bother them. Yes, even if they broke up with you, seeing you moving on will trigger something in them about wanting you back. They very likely did not expect you to pick up the pieces and go about life so quickly.

They will be impressed that you moved on so quickly and then, their self-esteem will take a blow because they will realize that if you moved on, maybe you did not value them as much as they thought!

Once they start thinking like that, you will be in control of the situation because once they start thinking that they want to be dating you again, and seeing how much fun you are having, it paves the way for the first contact.

10. Be Charismatic

This chapter is about harnessing the power of charisma to seduce your ex. Charisma is the factor that makes you instantly likeable. Charismatic people are charmers, the people who others just love to be around and by being charismatic, you will seduce your ex again.

Charismatic people are the people who you are just drawn to, they are nearly impossible to not enjoy talking to. Be charismatic and your ex will be eating out of your hand in no time.

Obviously, something was broken in your old relationship and if it reached the point where you broke up, communication was probably a factor. Or, perhaps you argued instead of having discussions.

Either way, there was anger or hurt on both sides and when emotions ran high, things may have been said that should never have been said. How do you erase your ex's memory of those words and of the arguments? With charisma, that is how.

Charisma allows you to communicate with your ex, without any of your past problems popping up. You will be charming, irresistible, and confident, which are all winning characteristics.

With charisma, you can charm people and they will be powerless. You have heard of the phrase 'to kill them with kindness'. That is how charisma works, only you seduce them with your charm instead. Kind words and a calm demeanor will get you things a temper tantrum will never achieve.

Charisma allows you to connect with other people better and because relationships are all about connecting with one another, you can use charisma to connect with your ex again, bridging the gap your breakup created.

Charisma is about how you say things and what you say. Instead of a demand, you ask a question. You give people choice to help you or to not help you but when you ask nicely, chances are that they will happily help you.

Instead of just making statements or giving orders, you speak so that the other person interacts with you, building a connection. For example, if you tell someone to get you a glass of water, they might say no and tell you to get it yourself.

However, if you ask it this way: "Would you mind getting me a glass of water please?" That request is softened and presented in a polite way and they will very likely get you your glass of water. You want to always be mindful of speaking in such a way that you get a positive result and that means that you are sincere, polite, and show empathy.

Another factor charismatic people have is that they are positive; no moaning, whining, or complaining when life is not going their way because they know that people do not want to hear about it. They know that life is not perfect but instead of bringing others down, they elevate the conversation into something more positive.

Some basics for being charismatic are:

#1 – Be Observant and Read People

Begin paying attention to body language when you talk to people so you can try to get an accurate read on their state of mind. Telling a joke to someone who is obviously not in the mood can work against you. Begin to get a feel for how people are feeling and then connect to them by showing empathy for whatever is going on and then work to help them get into a better place mentally.

Charismatic people do not walk away from people who need a kind word, they always seem to know when someone needs to have someone comfort them and they know by watching body language.

#2 – Be Animated

Start being more animated when you talk. Let your face and body language express your emotions as well as just what you are saying. People connect easier to people who are open with their emotions. Begin practicing being more animated and expressive.

#3 – Read Between the Lines

This goes hand-in-hand with the first lesson of being observant. A lot is said between the lines when you watch two people communicate. You can easily pick up on subtle clues on the dynamics of human interaction by simply paying attention to others. Knowing how to read between the lines of what is being said can give you a leg up when it comes to communicating better.

#4 - Keep Your Emotions in Check

Charismatic people do not fall apart when they are stressed, nor do they lash out in anger. You need to keep your emotions in check so that you do not project a negative image.

In addition, you have to know when to reel in your emotional responses so that they are appropriate. Some people joke when they are stressed or nervous but there are some situations where it is just callous and rude to do so. Learn to reel in your emotions so that you do not end up distancing yourself from anyone inadvertently. A calm demeanor and a good grasp on how and when you show emotions are vital.

In addition to the above, you need to communicate better than you ever have before. That means that you always say what you mean, you do not play word games, and you do it all with charm. Do not interrupt people, do not engage in pointless arguments, and leave your sarcasm at the door. Charisma means that you make a point to inquire about and talk about the lives of the people you are talking to.

Do not dominate the conversation about yourself, if someone asks you something personal, answer it and then steer the conversation back about the other person. When you show an interest in other people by not just asking about them but by actually listening to their answers and asking them to expand upon them, it shows that you are able to think about people other than yourself.

These skills are going to be very handy when you talk to your ex again because instead of making it all about you, you will be talking about them. You know what is going in your life and instead of telling them, you make them the center of the conversation. It shows that communicating with you will be better and easier than it used to be and that is another point in your favor.

11. First Contact

After three to four weeks of no contact, it is time for you to make first contact with your ex. Now, if your ex has contacted you, this chapter applies to that contact as well. No matter who contacts who, you need to be very careful in how your first contact goes because one wrong move here can be damaging to building a new relationship.

Ideally, they will contact you after seeing that you are going on with your life and having fun without them. But if they do not contact you first, after a month, it is time for you to prepare to initiate contact.

First, are you ready to make contact? Are you still angry about the break up? If so, you need to wait until you are no longer angry about the break up because otherwise, your anger will bleed into your words, your tone, and your actions and your ex will not want to talk to you.

Even if they were the one who was wrong, the minute you start blaming them or trying to argue about whose fault it was, you have lost them again. You have to be able to talk to them in a calm, positive, and polite manner.

Wow them with your charisma and your maturity during the first contact. If you argue or start becoming emotional, it will just remind them of all of the bad times you had together, especially at the end when all you did was fight.

You want to avoid that at all costs and that is why you need to be careful with how you communicate. Give them a positive experience and they will see the new you and be interested in communicating further.

If you have tried to constantly call them, with every phone call, they probably rolled their eyes at your persistence and ignored the call. However, you have gone a month without trying to contact them even once and so when you call, they will be interested in finding out what you want because they have not heard from you in a long while.

Do not text, email, or message on Facebook. You need to call them to make your first contact. If you know their working schedule, be careful to not call them during work hours, you want to call when you know they are not at work and able to talk. Pick a time when they are most likely to not be busy and to answer the phone.

Your goal is to not have a lengthy phone call. You do not want to just sit and chat on the phone, because you can seduce them easier in person. The entire point of the phone call is to try to get them to meet you in person. A simple meet up to say hello, that is all, nothing more and nothing less. Approach the idea as if it were two friends meeting up just to catch up.

This works because they will feel valued. It will please them that you still care and that you are showing it in a very mature and non-emotional manner. A short, pleasant phone call is probably the last thing your ex expected to receive from you. It will catch them off guard and it will intrigue them.

You have obviously changed if you are not sounding hurt or angry and you are not begging them to come back. This is subtle tactic to draw them back into your life slowly. Remember, you are about to start all over with your ex, a completely new chapter for the two of you. Your past relationship is toast so there is no need to bring it up.

The goal is to keep the phone call short, somewhere between five to ten minutes and no longer. You do not want there to be a chance to go into past issues nor do you want it to feel awkward. Already have a meeting place and time in mind, keeping in mind that it is a time that they should be available for. Make it a public place, like getting coffee at a café, or a quick lunch.

If you get their voicemail, leave a short message telling them that you just wanted to say hello and see how they are doing and then hang up. Wait for them to call back. Do not call daily. If they do not call after a week, try calling again and leaving a similar message, making sure it sounds happy and upbeat, short and sweet. Wait a week before trying again. If after four weeks you do not get a call back, chances are that you will not. However, this rarely happens.

If they say yes, mission accomplished and you can go to the next chapter, meeting up. If they say no or seem to hesitate, do not become discouraged because staying positive and calm is very important at this stage. If they sound hesitant or say that day or time does not work, just smoothly ask what time works before them. Casually say that it is only coffee and you just want to say hello. Tell them that it will just be for twenty minutes or so, so they know it will be short.

They usually say yes, because you are suggesting politely, instead of begging. Asking goes a long way. If they say no, tell them that you understand and politely end the conversation. Try again in a week, asking them if they would like to meet for a quick cup of coffee or a snack somewhere and see if you receive a better response. If you are told no three times, they will very likely not be interested in getting back together but at least you know that you are giving up on good terms and you never know what may happen.

12. Meeting Up

Your phone call worked and they have agreed to meet you, now what? You are well on your way to seducing your ex, showing them the new and improved you, so be careful to not be so eager that you blow it! Being too eager will translate as being needy and they will leave. You are not trying to obviously get them back. In fact, you aren't even going to mention it; doing so will ruin things.

You want them to come to you for a second chance. You want them to want to be with you again and this brief first meeting after the breakup will be how you do it. You want to be casual, fun, with no pressure or negativity. You want them to walk away from this meeting with nothing but positive thoughts about you and the encounter. You want them to want to see you again, which means you have to hold your emotions in check and play it cool.

Go for a light mood, no serious discussions, no talking about the past; you should be focused only on the present with no stress and no pressure. You want them back but they do not know that and you are not going to clue them in. Remember, hard to get is the way to go.

For the meeting, wear something new, not something they have seen you in before. It does not have to be a whole new outfit, maybe just a new top or pair of flattering pants. Take time to look good, show off your new hairstyle or color, and if you have lost weight, they will notice. The important thing is that you look rested, healthy, glowing, and confident.

All of those cosmetic self-improvements were to boost your confidence and now is your time to shine. When you walk through the front door, you need to radiate happiness and health. You want to have bright eyes, a genuine smile, and a positive vibe everyone in the room will notice.

You should shine from within as you walk in, your head held high, a smile on your lips, and exuding confidence. Without any hesitation, you will go up to your ex and tell them how good it is to see them and more importantly, thank them for meeting with you.

Instead of focusing on getting back together, focus on just enjoying the date. If your ex brings up your past relationship, steer it toward a positive memory. If they mention anything negative about the breakup, just counter with a memory of something fun you two did together. This is not the time to try to have a heavy discussion; you are just going to catch up like two people who have not seen each other in a while would do.

Do not try to be seductive or overly flirty, that will come later. Just be positive, upbeat, and fun. Do not mention seeing other people, how sad you were, or anything related to the breakup.

Avoid all heavy discussions about anything that can be negative. If they try to bring it up, steer the conversation to something positive. It is a good sign that they want to discuss the relationship but now is not the time.

The fact that you are deflecting any attempt to talk about the past helps you look like you have moved on and they will be even more intrigued. Continue to politely and cheerfully deflect any attempts on their part to bring up the relationship.

Talk about your job, your family, or even just the last movie you saw, anything but the relationship. Even though they are bringing up the relationship, they probably did not really want to discuss it so you are earning points with them by not talking about it.

Try to avoid physical contact during the date. However, use subtle body language to help them feel familiar with you and to trigger positive memories of you. Lean forward when you talk to them. It is too early in the game to try to rely on touching them, so try to avoid touching them if you can help it.

Smile, laugh, lean closer, and make sure that your body language is loose and relaxed. If you are uptight and nervous, it will show through and they will end up being nervous as well, and unable to just relax around you.

You told them that it would just be twenty minutes or a half hour so when the time is up, end the date. Even if things are going well, you need to end the date.

Do not ask to meet again at this stage but do make sure to thank them for meeting with you and tell them that you really enjoyed seeing them again. Do not try to hug, kiss, or even touch them first; if they lean in for a hug or a kiss, then you can give them a brief hug or kiss but let them initiate it. Never initiate touch on the first date.

Leave on a positive note, looking happy and acting confident. Even if your heart is hammering, walk out with your head held high and with pep in your step. Your ex will see how pleasant it was to see you again and it will bring up all of the old, positive memories they have of you. This is exactly what you want.

13. The Next Step

Your initial reaction is probably that because the first meeting went so well, you should immediately set up a second meeting. You need to continue to play hard to get and not show how desperate you are to get back together. If your ex calls you and wants to see you again, congratulations on a job well done. You are only a few happy dates from seducing your ex and getting back together.

See if they text, call, or begin emailing you again. If so, that is a very good sign and just keep all communications short and positive. Continue to avoid discussing anything related to the past relationship. After a week, ask them to meet with you again. If you have been in contact during the last week, you will probably receive an immediate yes. If you have not been in contact, your chances of them saying yes are very good.

Because you did not hound them after meeting up and the first meeting went so smoothly and positive, they will very likely tell you yes. After all, you gave them every reason to say yes and not a single reason to tell you no. Just like before, suggest a date, time, and place for another get together but instead of coffee, think of something fun to do.

Avoid going to the movies, or to dinner, because it is too early in the get back together game for you to be place in an intimate setting with your ex. Find something local and fun to do, such as a zoo, a comedy show, go see a band, a fair, or even an amusement park. You want to go do something in public, surrounded by many people so that the date feels casual. If they say no, then ask them out for another coffee or lunch instead.

You want to create an environment of fun by creating new memories. You are helping yourself appear as someone fun to be around. Wherever you go, make sure to have fun! Just like before, avoid the topic of your relationship. This is your chance to start building up fun new memories to overshadow any negative memories of you and your past relationship.

Make sure to pass out a few compliments to your ex, tell them how good they look but make it genuine and do not hand out compliments too heavy handed, just one or two compliments per date.

During this second date, make a point to very lightly touch the back of their hand when you are talking and then move your hand quickly. Using a quick but light touch is a very intimate gesture but it is a very familiar gesture and it helps them reconnect with you.

Do the light touch once or twice during this second date, always when you are laughing or talking about something happy or positive. Quick light touches are perfect ways to use non-verbal behavior in a non-pressured way.

End the second date just like the first one, on a happy and positive note. If they did not pull away from your light touches to their hand, end this date with a brief hug and then tell them how much fun you had.

By now, they will probably be calling you to keep in contact, which is just what you want. Continue going on casual dates for about a month before taking a bigger step to a more intimate setting, which would be the movies or dinner. Movies and dinner is the cliché dating activity for a reason, you are in a more intimate setting and it is more romantic. If you have had a successful run of fun dates, it is time to take it up a notch.

Ask them about dinner and a movie and suggest a movie, date, and time. Pick a movie you know they will be interested in; this is time for you to cater to their movie tastes, not yours. Continue to use the no pressure and no stress feel for the date. After the movie, go to dinner. Take their arm or put your arm around them when you are walking up to the restaurant, making it seem like a very casual and natural act. If they allow you to do so, it is time for the next step.

When you are eating, ask them casually if they would like to date exclusively because things are going well. Be sure to tell them how much you have enjoyed spending time with them and that you have been very happy. By now, they will probably be very open, especially because you have not put any pressure on them and you have not brought up the past once.

If they are not sure, act like it is no big deal, change the subject, and just continue to have fun with them. The more time they spend with you in a positive light, the more they will want to be back together with you. Just continue to take it one date at a time but in between dates, be sure to call them every day or so just to ask how they are and to listen and respond to what is going on in their life.

People love it when people care about them and by showing you care, even though they said no to getting back together, they will begin to realize what they are missing.

When they say yes, congratulations, you have successfully seduced your ex and gotten them back. Now, you must avoid the pitfalls from the first relationship. You will not get a third chance, so make sure you do not repeat the same mistakes. You can build a healthy relationship as long as you trust and respect each other.

14. Conclusion

Break ups are always bad; they hurt. It is even worse when you want your ex back. You can seduce your ex and get them back, providing you follow the plan in this book. Being needy, desperate, or constantly wanting to talk about the past relationship will derail your ability to get back together.

Avoid placing blame or asking them to forgive you for something you have done. You want to avoid reminding them of any bad parts from the past, which is why you have to build a whole new you. You want to show them that you able to forge a strong relationship with them and that it can be fun.

Patience is the key toward getting your ex back. Patience and a calm demeanor will get you back into their lives. By presenting a positive outlook and personality, you will be showing them a better side of you and you can easily seduce your ex right back into your life.

www.ingramcontent.com/pod-product-compliance
Ingram Content Group UK Ltd.
Pitfield, Milton Keynes, MK11 3LW, UK
UKHW041915190726
13854UKWH00003B/1263

9 781304 994516